Fixing Broken Buildings

Why Our Buildings are Crumbling

Building Better Bridges Today to Create the Healthy Buildings of Tomorrow

Dimitri Livas

ISBN 13: 978-0-9876338-9-7

2

CONTENTS

PART ONE

About This Book

Hello and welcome. I'm Dimitri Livas and it's a pleasure to have you here.

This book is essentially a collection of articles, essays and opinion pieces borne of 25 years of experience in the construction industry, with 20 of those years as the founder and CEO of the Savil Group: a successful commercial construction company specialising in the repair, restoration, conservation, and remediation of broken buildings. On these pages you'll find an investigation into why our buildings are crumbling and why our infrastructure is broken.

I'll begin our journey into the world of broken buildings by laying some foundations: in this case that means exploring what it takes to fix broken buildings and also what's required to create healthy ones in the first place. That includes my perspective on the having the right systems and partnerships in place to ensure buildings are taken care of.

Then I'll get specific as I share my thoughts on some of the most notorious cases of broken buildings and infrastructures throughout Australia and the world, as well as honing in on the particular issues facing the construction industry today.

The final part of the book examines the tell-tale signs that a building is in need of attention and care. I'll lift the lid on how we work at Savil, and I'll offer advice on what to look out for if you're in the position of needing to hire a company to take care of your buildings.

I'm thrilled to be here and to be able to share what I know and have learnt these past 25 years with you. I'll begin by telling you a little more about why this book means so much to me.

Why Broken Buildings?
My Story

Construction gets me excited. Problem-solving gets me excited. Business gets me excited. Helping people gets me excited. I love leading people, and I love learning new things. I love talking, presenting, sharing and connecting.

Like most entrepreneurs with a long career, I've ridden the waves of both success and hardship, weathering dozens of storms and learning invaluable lessons along the way.

Going right back to my childhood I was the typical kid with a car wash round — but not so typical in that I had to employ a couple of friends to help me manage the demand! I got such a buzz from leading that small team, generating local business and satisfying our customers. Moreover, the fulfilment that came with being self-sufficient hooked me in and has never let me go.

The truth is, I've always been ambitious by nature. Even back then I had an inner knowing that I'd forge my own path in life and always work for myself.

But I've never been afraid of getting my hands dirty either. In my teens that meant learning the building trade from the ground up. I worked on construction sites, immersing myself in the work and acquiring the knowledge that would lead me to run my own sites and projects in the future.

The 'future' came pretty fast: in my early twenties I purchased, renovated and turned around a run-down restaurant in central Canberra — while also studying for my Bachelor of Commerce and an Advanced Diploma in Construction Management at University.

I worked flat-out to make the restaurant a success
— and though the whole process was something of
a baptism of fire, it laid the foundations of all that
would follow.

With my first-hand construction experience and
real-world business expertise it made perfect sense
that I'd start my own construction company. Savil
has been in operation for 20 years, starting out with
just me and a handful of trusted friends and
collaborators — many of whom are still with me
today — though now we're a core team of twelve
with hundreds of contractors working alongside us.

In essence, we do two things at Savil: We Fix
Broken Buildings, and we create healthy ones too.
We're experts in repairing major structural damage
and modernising buildings to improve their use,
beauty and investment value.

We've won multi-million dollar projects for some of
Australia's biggest brands, and I'm incredibly proud

of all we continue to achieve and how we continue to grow.

Now you've got a better picture of me and what I'm about, let's get to the meat of the book. In the following chapter I'll lay out the basics of what it takes to fix broken buildings, before leading into how we can create and maintain healthy buildings.

Lets dive in!

Fixing Broken Buildings:
The Basics

In essence, there are three key questions that help us to determine the state and health of a building:

Was it designed well?
Was it built well?
Is it being well looked after?

All three questions and the answers they lead us to will help shine a light on what's contributing to the current state of any building.

Imagine an old, beat up, rusty car. Picture it: maybe it's parked up on some wasteland, windows smashed, weeds growing around it. It's very likely this car was abandoned and it hasn't been used for years.

Now, what if that car is a 1967 Mustang? What if it

started out as a breath-taking piece of machinery and engineering?

It had immaculate paint work, beautiful upholstery, and it ran like a dream. The kind of car that demanded admiring glances everywhere it went. Because its first careful owner took great care of it, all three boxes were ticked for a while: it was designed well, made well, and it was looked after.

But then the car changed hands and the next owner was less careful, then less interested, then not motivated at all to carry out even basic maintenance. The thing is, no matter how well the car was designed and built, it still required some care: the oil and timing belts needed to be changed occasionally, and the tyres too.

And what happens if the new owner drove it like a race car everyday? It can't withstand such treatment: it will break, and it'll break sooner and on a bigger scale than a car that's been looked after.

Just like the car, buildings are affected by wear and tear. They can be designed well, built well, but they still have parts that need replacing and paint that fades away under our strong sun and biting frost.

Essentially, they still need to be taken care of. I'll be getting deeper into this as the book progresses by looking at the specific issues, defects and calls for attention that show a building requires repair.

For the moment, I'd like to delve into the subject of healthy buildings and what it takes to build, fix and maintain them.

Creating Healthy Buildings
A Retelling of The Three Little Pigs

(Or: Why We Need To Create Healthy Buildings)

Now I presume you know the story of the three little pigs: one pig built a house straw (spoiler: it didn't last), his brother built a house of sticks (see previous spoiler) and the third little pig built a house of bricks. Now *that* was a house built to last. Clever little pig with his bricks. Have you ever wondered what became of him?

Well, Gary (that was his name, in case you missed that in the original fairytale) settled down and married another pig, Sally, who was a designer. Soon they had three little piglets of their own: Joey, Loui and baby Mary.

As solid and homely as their much-loved house of bricks was, the truth was Gary and his family had to sell up and move to the city to find work. With urban density increasing, the family found themselves in an apartment tower in the city — a world away from the solid, bespoke and dependable home Gary had built.

And so the little piglets, Joey, Loui and Mary, grew up listening to Mum and Dad endlessly complaining about the state of the building they lived in. "Whoever designed this balcony drainage system should be shot," Sally would say, with Gary adding, "Well, yeah but it goes beyond the design — whoever *built* this endlessly leaking sieve should be made into pork chops."

Because the piglets grew up listening to their parents bemoan the work of builders, all three decided that they would never go into that particular line of work. But they were still interested in and inspired by construction, so, the first little piggy

Joey, became a property developer, while the second little piggy, Loui, became a building consultant. Mary, the third little piggy, became a town planner. As each piglet grew into an adult pig they all made their way into the world.

Joey, the developer, moved to Lawson, where he decided to build his first lot of units. Now, Joey was shrewd and cunning. In truth, he'd taken after his uncle (Mr House of Straw, who was fond of shortcuts) and the reason he chose to build in Lawson was because he knew the council had a really easy approval process. He worked with a designer who gave him a bare-bones basic design, the minimum needed for approval, and he used his superior negotiating skills to hustle with a builder that could build it fast and cheap. Finally he found a certifier who was too busy to do detailed inspections. Joey was all set to reap the profits of the sales and live in one of the units of the tower block. What could possibly go wrong?

Well, because this story is about the Three Little Pigs, you won't be too surprised to know that the Big Bad Wolf is never far away. And we all know that Mr Big Bad loves to beat his chest and huff and puff and blow houses down? Well, when he came for Joey's tower block, he didn't even bother knocking on the door; he already knew from experience that no self-respecting pig would ever let him in. So he used what he had: he huffed and he puffed and he conjured up a storm with wind, rain, and a whole lot of hail.

Well, guess what happened to Joey's units? The wet seal on the balconies failed and leaked. The roof let the rain in easily and water flooded into the living areas and bedrooms. Light fittings short-circuited, and pandemonium ensued.

Needless to say the unit owners wanted to string Joey up and turn him into pork sausages, but Joey (being the shrewd bugger that he was) wound up the company and ran away from Lawson to stay with his brother Loui — Loui who'd become a building consultant.

Now, Loui lived in a town called Belco, and in Belco Loui had gained a bit of experience as The Man Who Fixed Broken Buildings. He knew about what had happened with the towers in Lawson and so when he had his turn at developing an apartment tower he was careful not to make the same mistakes as those developers.

Loui made sure that he hired a very reputable and established builder, along with a good certifier and experienced engineers. It wasn't until he was totally ready, with all his ducks in a row, that he started building.

Once the build was underway, the town planners, much more 'on it' than those in Lawson, came and checked that Loui hadn't made changes to the plans without lodging an amendment. You could say he did everything to the letter.

Only doing everything to the letter would be this little pig's downfall: because when some of the contractors told him that they thought the design had flaws, he instructed them to build it as per the plans, insisting he'd done his homework, and that the contractors should stick to the job remit and stop hunting for variations.

So much for having a proper feedback loop! But if Loui had a fault it's that he was stubborn, and he thought he'd taken enough measures to ensure his build would be safe and a success. On the surface it was: he built a beautiful tower with a bright and shiny facade of composite aluminium cladding with a polythylene core that stretched all the way to the sky, and things seemed fine for a while.

But this is the story of the Three Little Pigs, so it wasn't long before The Big Bad Wolf came a-knocking. And once he arrived, Big Bad was relentless. Not content with a couple of random storms, he started visiting once a week. And before long, water started to find its way through the roof and into the ceilings of the penthouse units. Soon, the louvres would start to rattle and shake on the side of the building, but the executive committee dug its heels in and wouldn't pay to maintain it, until one day, tragedy struck: one of the louvres finally blew off the building almost killing a passerby.

And then to top it all off, Big Bad, in a fit of excitement, jumped up and down stamping his feet, causing a minor, almost undetectable Earthquake — but just enough to give the building's foundations a little more settlement than usual, and shearing one of the concrete columns in the car park.

The next day everyone who lived in a direct line above that column — all 20 floors — couldn't open their front door without kicking it out, because the frames had moved. But, if that wasn't enough, Big Bad, who loved to smoke cigars, flicked his ashes onto the facade and the building went up in flames.

Joey and Loui, with their dubious moral compass and questionable ethics, squealed in panic, then packed their bags and did a runner: this time jumping onto a plane and flying to Germany where their sister, Mary, lived.

Now, Mary was a successful town planner in the city of Casey — and in Casey they'd got it right. In Casey the construction industry had and was subject to:

- Effective planning and approvals
- Real feedback between the government and industry
- Check and stop points in both the design and the build phase (especially on the main culprits such as wet seal systems, installation, and balcony designs)
- Well-documented maintenance systems
- An education programme for the executive committees and strata managers so they

understood how to look after their buildings and keep them healthy

So when Joey and Loui asked Mary, "Why don't you have issues with your buildings, Mary?" she replied, "We all work together to create healthy buildings, and even though Big Bad comes several times a year, he never gets the better of us here."

And the moral of this fun little story is… we need to create healthy buildings! From the ground up.

For those curious about what happened to Joey and Loui — well, they where tracked down by the ATO and extradited back to Australia for not paying their taxes. Needless to say, they got sent to the pig pen for a while.

What is it that worked for Mary in Casey? It all came down to systems: the right systems were in place — ones that take into account the full life of the building from its initial inception to its eventual demolition.

Let's explore how those systems might look next.

Getting The Right Systems In Place And Building Better Bridges

Creating and maintaining healthy buildings requires a multifaceted approach. We need to consider what will impact on the health of the building as it's constructed, and we need to look beyond that initial construction phase and into the life of the building once it's in use.

It should go without saying that the creation of a healthy building starts in the construction of that building, which is why, when something goes wrong the finger of blame is usually pointed at the builder.

In some cases this is fair, but it doesn't paint the full picture, and without painting a full picture, we might be blind to the repair and remediation that's actually required.

Earlier in the book, I asked you think about an old,

beat up car which hasn't run well — if at all — for years. Then I asked you to imagine that car was a 1967 Mustang which started out its life as a beautiful looking car when it came off the factory floor — just like our shiny new buildings do.

Let's expand on this analogy for a moment. If, in the first couple of years the design of the car is found to have some flaws, the factory operations team (the building part of the process) make adjustments to improve and solve those issues.

How well the car is maintained and looked after comes down to how much care the driver has for it, and how good his or her mechanic is.

Alongside this, there's a feedback loop: customers offer complaints and feedback to Mustang, and dealers and mechanics will do the same. A good company will adjust the design, and improve its operations to iron out the flaws.

Our buildings are no different to cars.

Healthy buildings are a product of their design, their build, and how they're maintained. In this way, all three ingredients work together to create healthy buildings.

But we also have to look beyond these elements, towards effective connections and communication between government and industry. This is a key element of taking care of broken buildings and creating healthy ones.

How the government and the construction industry can work together to create healthy buildings

1. Strata managers and owners' corporations should be required to partner with qualified asset managers, and companies that understand construction

One problem that seems to persist is a lack of action in the early days of building issues being identified by owners corporations and strata managers. This might come down to indecision, lack of understanding of the process, or lack of skill and proper direction from consultants. It's worthwhile to note that most owners' corporations are made up of owners who simply volunteer their time, so they're not always qualified to manage a building with major issues.

A qualified asset manager should team up with a company that understands construction and has at their fingertips a whole host of remedies for any issues, and the networks and the means to carry out the necessary work — and to educate the stakeholders in those buildings. That's what ensures buildings have a healthy life.

2. Employ inspectors who have enough time and resources to do their job properly

In fact — I'd recommend impartial structural engineers to be involved in a build from Day One. We can look to Dubai for inspiration here — a city which has some of the world's largest and most impressive structures (built on sand, of all things). They have additional measures in place during construction where the structural engineer is impartial and their decision is independent. They also have the authority to actually stop the works and stop the concrete pouring if there's a concern.

3. Place a stronger focus on the main risk and problem areas of waterproofing, cladding fire safety, concrete and steel reinforcements

In essence, we need as many eyes checking works as possible. Again in Dubai, government authorities have their own engineer to conduct inspections in addition to the structural engineers and the builders' engineers. These additional inspections

ensure that nothing slips through the gaps —
whether it's an honest mistake or the result of a
lack of resourcing or incompetence.

**4. Introduce specialist consultants who perform
a preventative rather than a prescriptive role**
This entails consultants working on a build who
have the expertise to prevent future issues
occurring, rather than being brought in after
something has gone wrong to prescribe the fix. An
example would be a wet seal consultant being
closely involved with the build who has to sign off
and document each stage of the wet seal process
during construction — according to legislation that
is both clear and effective.

**5. Have tighter regulations in the design
process and in the build process**
Along with this, I'd like to see increased level of
government oversight when it comes to inspections

of works in progress, especially in the higher risk structural parts of the works. Fire safety and issues around water such as wet sealing, water ingress and water failure should also be prioritised.

6. Protection for the buyer in the case of major defects

Buyers need legislative protection, and the creation of such laws would need to be made in collaboration with the government's regulatory authorities, industry construction specialists, and bodies such as the Master Builders Association (MBA) who push for a quality of build. I'd also recommend ongoing professional development, education, and adherence to standards for members of the MBA.

The crux of all of this is: the more people who understand the true needs of both government and industry, the better bridges we can create between these worlds. This is essential to ensure the safety, the use, and the longevity of our buildings.

Let's move into Part Two of the book now, and apply some of what we've looked at so far as I share my specific thoughts on how to handle, fix and look to the future in some of the most notorious and interesting cases of broken buildings and infrastructure around the world.

PART TWO

The Quality Of New Apartment Buildings:

A Crisis In The Construction Industry

If there's one debate that's front and centre in the construction industry right now it's the quality of new apartment buildings. Buildings are being scrutinised more than ever — thanks to those highly publicised examples of things going terribly wrong — many of which will be covered on the pages of this book.

This chapter gives an overview of the types of issues we're seeing in modern apartment complexes and the causes of these issues. We'll look at how they're affecting owners, investors, residents and the Australian economy in general. We'll also discuss how these problems can be fixed, and how we can learn from our mistakes so we can create healthier buildings in the future.

The three most common issues

1. Sinking or shifting buildings

This issue is all too often brought to our attention when large cracks appear in the concrete of a structure — or, perhaps more alarmingly — when we hear the concrete cracking — as residents of Sydney's Opal Tower did in 2018. Naturally, questions were asked about how this could happen, questions which then lead us to wonder whether corners were cut in an attempt to cut costs for the builders and developers.

We'll look more closely at what happened at the Opal Tower in a later chapter, but for now I'll say that one report cited the following as potential causes to its structural issues: changes made to the original design of the complex, poorly designed critical support beams, and the use of "low-strength" concrete.

More recently, cracks were found in another Sydney residential block, Mascot Towers. The appearance of these large cracks led to an engineer's report which found the building to be "moving in a downward motion."

Again, this is a case I'll be unpacking later in the book. At the time of writing, the exact cause in the case of Mascot Towers is still unknown and investigations are continuing.

Even though Mascot is around ten years older than Opal, it seems like growing speculation points to a similar set of circumstances as those in the Opal Tower case, and that speculation is pointing at poor design and construction practices. In Mascot's case it also seems there was a lack of maintenance over its young life, so the combination of this trio: design, construction and maintenance, resulted in a poor quality building which poses a serious safety risk.

2. Major water leaks

Another common issue plaguing owners in new apartment buildings is major water leaks. In new buildings this is usually a result of builders or developers using cheaper suppliers, products, and sub-contractors to try and lower costs.

A classic example of this is poor waterproofing, sometimes brought on by a rush to meet a hand-over deadline. Couple that with using a shoddy sub-contractor and then finally a lack of proper supervision and what you get is something along the lines of terribly inadequate wet sealing on balconies which allows water to leak into the apartments, sometimes flooding them completely.

Often, water leaks point to dodgy plumbing or larger building defects, and these have a knock-on effect on a building's plumbing system.

A jaw-dropping example of this was highlighted in the news in 2017, when a resident of Wentworth

Point in Sydney had a dam installed in his living room. Yes — you read that right! A dam to try to control the 120 litres of water that flooded his apartment during spells of heavy rain. This was something he put in place when the owner was advised that any legal proceedings against the developer would be lengthy and costly. And so this desperate resident installed a dam — which he has to vacuum out each time it rains — while he waits to find out the outcome of his case.

This oh-so common water leak crisis has even got a name; it's been labelled "leaky building syndrome" in a report by the Victorian Building Authority, where an inquiry found that waterproofing is a "systemic issue".

3. High-risk cladding and fire safety

Another tragically common issue is non-compliant and high-risk cladding: a world-wide problem that we've seen too often in the news in the last few years, most notably with the 2017 Grenfell Tower fire in London. Thankfully, regulations are catching up in some Australian states as laws are passed to prevent the use of flammable cladding. However, the complex battle to remove and replace cladding on affected buildings still continues. Again, this is an issue I'll be exploring in depth as the book progresses.

Problems with combustible cladding have also shone a spotlight on another long standing problem in both new and older apartment buildings: the issue of inadequate fire safety protection. It's understandable for older buildings, which aren't regularly inspected and updated correctly, to fall below the line of adequate fire safety protection — but for this to be a common issue in new apartment buildings is just mind-boggling.

How is all of this affecting the construction industry in Australia?

The fact is, the Australian building industry is suffering the effects of these extremely low quality new apartment buildings, to the extent that we have a situation which some experts are labelling a serious "crisis of confidence" for buyers and investors. That's a worrying statement: it means that buying an apartment in a new building is no longer considered a "safe" option.

The deeper truth is that there's not only a loss of confidence in the building industry, but also in statutory warranty laws and consumer protections in Australia.

Stephen Goddard, spokesperson for the strata owners' advocacy group, the Owners' Corporation Network, believes that approximately 80 per cent of all new apartment buildings are constructed with structural defects. Now that's a big call, and I'm not sure how the word "structural" is being used in this instance, but there are many defects we can't ignore and the truth is most of them won't surface until the six year statutory warranty period has passed.

One thing that's also important to add here is that many owners and owners' corporations are not aware of how to effectively manage a problem building. This only works to compound all of the issues we're examining here. A lot of buyers are becoming hesitant to buy new apartments, to the point that it's becoming more appealing to purchase properties that are more than ten years old — because there's a good chance that any major defects will have become apparent in this time frame.

Far-reaching consequences

This loss of confidence in new developments affects investors, who then start looking to take their developments elsewhere. This has a snowball effect on the Australian economy, hitting the construction industry hard.

Moreover, there's the more immediate impact on owners and residents — those who are stranded when major defects in their buildings leave them without a home for indeterminable periods of time.

How can such a widespread problem be best handled? As with all highly publicised events, particularly in cases where the inhabitants of highly populated buildings such as these are left without accommodation, the public often looks to the government for answers.

When asked to comment on the Opal Tower situation, NSW Premier Gladys Berejiklian told the public that she wanted to see "legislation overhauling the building industry" introduced in the next session of Parliament.

In the more recent case of Mascot Towers, the Federal Industry Minister, Karen Andrews, called for "consistent certification standards" for building surveyors and certifiers while pointing to and highlighting a loss of confidence in the building sector.

This confidence must be restored — because no one wants structurally unsound buildings, unsafe buildings, defective buildings or leaking buildings to be the norm in our society.

Looking ahead

The government has now committed to implementing reforms that will overhaul the construction industry, but with higher density living increasing and more and more apartment buildings springing up all over the country, there's valid concern that these changes can't happen soon enough to protect new owners. At the time of writing, there's no clear indication of when these reforms — and that means effective reforms — will be passed in parliament.

As we wait for more answers in the case of Mascot

Towers, and as the Opal Tower owners fight for remediation works, the rest of the building industry is looking at how we can learn from these mistakes and create healthy buildings in the future.

It seems the government is in the process of taking the first step, but more needs to be done at both a government level and at the ground level of designers, builders, certifiers and developers. As we look more closely at what can be done here, we need to go beyond Australia and look to the rest of the world, to those countries already creating healthy buildings and creating positive change in the building industry. Then we can apply these lessons in practical, effective and efficient ways to build better buildings.

Because wouldn't that be the ideal?

The Sydney And Melbourne Buildings: A Lesson For Us All

I love the Sydney and the Melbourne buildings in Canberra. They're twins, built exactly the same, in 1927.

These are two of Canberra's most historic buildings — two jewels in our crown, so to speak. And yet, one of those buildings, The Sydney Building, has been in a terrible state for years.

For various reasons it's unkempt, not looked after, ignored and downright dangerous. It's suffered two major fires in the space of ten years: one which had a blast so strong that it sent a shop keeper hurtling across the street.

The blaze consumed virtually half the building — a building that couldn't keep up with basic code changes to fire regulation, and that failed to have fire separation between the units.

This heritage building, whose original design was based on the grand colonnades of St Mark's Square in Venice, is not only an unsightly mess — it's life threatening.

Take then its sister across the street: revived, renewed and brought back to life. The Melbourne Building is so much more inviting. It adds value to the community, and the community use it. On top of that, the unit owners are happy because business is good. Isn't that the ideal scenario?

So, how can we learn from this?
Essentially, the Sydney Building requires attention and care. It's a prime example of how necessary it is that we look after our buildings. A remediation company is required to navigate this complex web

of issues, and to reinstate the Sydney Building as a piece of architecture Canberra can be proud of once again.

The Opal Tower:
A Fateful Eight Seconds

On Christmas Eve 2018, the residents of Sydney's Opal Tower experienced something unsettling and really quite terrifying: a loud, structural creaking noise was heard from within their apartment building.

If you're not familiar with The Opal Tower, it's a 36-storey residential building forming part of the redevelopment of the famous Olympic Park. With its unique triangular design and million dollar apartments, the Opal Tower is — or was — a highly regarded piece of architecture. Moreover — it's new, very new: the building had been in use for less than a year when this alarming event happened.

Not surprisingly, that creaking noise sent

shockwaves through the building industry as well as the lives of the people living in the tower. It lasted a full eight seconds, the same amount of time as a magnitude 7.0 earthquake.

Luckily, all residents remained safe — though many chose not to remain in the Opal Tower. Afraid the building would collapse, concerned residents immediately evacuated the tower and many moved out indefinitely.

In the immediate aftermath of this event, the owners' corporation made a deal with the developer, Ecove, to extend the warranty on the tower from twelve to 36 months, and investigations were opened.

Along with this, the NSW Department of Planning commissioned Unisearch, the engineering group, to investigate and produce an interim report. The seventeen page document found that the Opal Tower was structurally sound — which I'm sure offered some relief for those affected — but it's clear that the tower still requires significant rectification works.

The developer, Ecove, has spent in excess of ten million dollars rectifying the damage, and they're likely to spend a whole lot more. Some of those initial costs included relocating and reimbursing residents while investigations were carried out. Furthermore there's the necessary financial burden of diagnosing the extent of the issues and the creation and implementations of a plan for rectification with the builder.

My heart goes out to the unit owners and the residents. Buying a home is one of the biggest and most exciting investments of many people's lives, and the unit owners are facing nothing but distress, uncertainty, and likely financial ruin. It's no exaggeration to say the Opal Tower's fall from grace is literally a symbol of the biggest Australian dream gone totally and utterly wrong.

So, what happened?

It transpired that the loud, heavy creaking sound came as a result of heavy cracks developing in precast concrete slabs and panels on the tenth floor of the tower. Further investigations have found more cracks, this time in the precast concrete walls.

Beyond that, a variety of other issues have been identified, including burst support beams, dodgy patch-up jobs, more slabs riddled with cracks, precast concrete panels with shear cracks and peeling concrete, large cracks along the ceilings, under-designed horizontal beams, non-compliant grout between the beams and the concrete panels, and other defects as defined through the national construction code and the Australian Standards. It seems like everything that could go wrong within those mere eight seconds has.

The situation now

At the time of writing, nearly half of the tower's 392 apartments are still in a state deemed not habitable, while hundreds of floor to ceiling props have been installed to stabilise the structure and the structural elements. Right now there's no clear timeline for when the residents of these units can return to their apartments. Even the go-ahead for the initial rectification works has only just been given by the owner's body corporate, a whole four months after those cracks made themselves known.

Some thoughts

I can only imagine the frustrations of everyone affected, and while four months might seem like a long period of time, the truth is, rectifications *do* take time — especially when you're dealing with the kind of issues that have been discovered at the Opal Tower.

It's essential to source the right people to

investigate such a serious situation properly: to pore through the infinite lists of documentation, to probe contractors, to test materials, to open up areas for inspections, and ultimately to design a way forward that takes into account how to fix the issues so that they don't come up again, while also ensuring that the building can be managed and maintained into the long future.

Add into the mix that there's a very bright spotlight shining on this tower, while people across the industry — legitimately — question why and how this happened.

It's useful to keep in mind that the Unisearch report is an interim report, and the situation would benefit from a variety of experts conducting more investigations to determine a full diagnosis and to provide a full scope of works for remedy. Towers and buildings of this magnitude can be really dangerous if structurally unsound and if they're not managed properly. They are complex pieces of architecture with many facets, needs and requirements.

From what I've learned about this saga, it's clear to me that the steel hob beams used to reinforce the concrete need to be repaired and strengthened. The main question, however, is one of scope: what's the full scope of works required, and the magnitude of the repairs? And will the repairs only be carried out on the floors initially affected, or will the engineers determine, through their investigations and future risk mitigation strategies, that repairs should be applied to all the steel hob beams throughout the tower? This is a possibility, considering the fact that there were elements of the building that were found to be under-designed. Depending on the builder and the style of contract entered into with the developer, the design is usually what the builder relies upon and works from to create the structure.

In such large structures the design process itself is

almost as complicated, if not more, than the construction process — and it's certainly just as important to get it right, which is likely why Unisearch have recommended that independent structural engineers are engaged to check the final proposals in detail before major rectification works begin.

It should be noted that the Opal Tower isn't the only building in Australia to suffer these sort of defects and controversies. Some recent examples include the 22-storey Chelsea Tower in Chatswood which suffered leaks, cracked and peeling render, and corrosion. There's also the World Tower in Sydney with its flooding issues and faulty fire systems, and the Lacrosse Tower in Melbourne's Docklands which hit the news after combustible cladding had fire rocketing up one side of the building. I'll be examining the combustible cladding crisis later in the book.

Looking ahead

There are many people and players involved in the rectification works at the Opal Tower, from architects to structural engineers, hydraulics engineers, electrical, mechanical and acoustic engineers, all the way to town planners, certifiers and local councils.

It's essential that effective and efficient feedback loops are put in place to communicate issues that arise on the coal face. Proper hold points are required during construction for detailed review and feedback from qualified engineers.

Without these measures in place, problems can slip through unseen, and in a structure like this it doesn't take much for a small issue to be magnified to huge one. One example might be the support beams bursting — in this case because they weren't designed properly and were supported by under-strength concrete, and other deficiencies in the building materials.

Major works will be completed on levels four to ten, however 105 apartments spread throughout all floors will be directly affected. Although the investigating engineers WSP and the builder have stated that the building is structurally sound, residents are reluctant to move back in — and it's easy to see why. From being concerned about the safety of their children around construction rectification works, to the general safety of the building, there's also the inconvenience of constant construction works and living on what would effectively be a construction site.

Is there a light at the end of the tunnel for the residents, the owners, the builders, engineers, developers, state government and everyone involved in the ongoing saga of the Opal Tower tragedy? Only time will tell, but in all honesty it's difficult to imagine the building escaping the black cloud that now hovers over it.

Is the problem bigger than one building?

I have to say, from my experience: yes. In fact, in a few chapters time I'll talk about a similar situation at Mascot Towers, also in Sydney.

The truth is, the issues found at the Opal Tower are far too common. Though this case is in the public eye and has gained international attention, there are thousands of buildings just in Australia with similar defects. Not all of them hit the spotlight because those involved — and responsible — would rather work out what's going on behind the scenes if they can.

Part of the issue is the speed at which construction is happening; that makes it hard for the government regulators to keep up. Certifiers and inspectors are overloaded with work. Simply — resources are limited, people are stretched, and cases aren't managed properly.

Furthermore, there's the varying quality of builders, designers, and subcontractors. When buildings go up with such haste, substandard work is more likely.

The whole situation is stressful not only for the owners of these buildings, but for the subcontractors who are trying to do the right thing. They're competing with people who will bow to the demand by cutting corners on quality and on safety.

The key areas where change is required

Tighter regulations — in all areas

There's no denying that we need to tighten our building regulations. Everyone can see that. What some people miss, however, is the need to broaden our perspective to include tighter regulations not just for builders but also designers, subcontractors, inspectors and engineers. There are a lot more parties involved in actually getting buildings designed, put up, and then maintained. They need to be subject to closer scrutiny too.

Education for buyers

Buyers need that bigger picture view too: they need to know how to choose a reputable designer and builder and also how to choose a reputable certifier — especially for smaller buildings. In those cases buyers have a lot of control, and they can ensure the quality of a build at every stage of the process and into future maintenance.

Let's hope those involved in fixing the Opal, and all of the broken buildings in Australia and beyond, can co-ordinate the right people and teams to find the real problem, report them clearly and get the works done right.

The Problem With Level Crossings

We're taking a temporary side step from buildings now and into infrastructure, as we look at level crossings: those notorious spaces where a railway line intersects with a road at street level. I'm keen to examine level crossings because they're part of a broken and outdated railway system, and, moreover — they present a real danger to drivers, passengers, and pedestrians.

One such notorious crossing was, until very recently, located at High Street, Reservoir, in Melbourne. With 36,000 vehicles travelling through the crossing every day, and with the boom gates coming down frequently and for extended periods of time — especially during peak morning traffic — it's no surprise that this crossing was the cause of major traffic congestion across all of Melbourne.

What's worse, and more worrying, is that in the last

ten years alone this crossing was responsible for three recorded collisions, 26 near-misses and a fatality.

The problem doesn't begin and end with the crossing in Reservoir; this is a nationwide, and global, issue. In early 2019 a 70-year-old woman was killed on the tracks at a level crossing in Queensland. This highlights just how dangerous level rail crossings are. Beyond the fact that they cause major traffic congestion, they also cause collisions, and in severe cases, fatalities.

The question is, what's being done to fix this broken infrastructure? And is it enough?

The current situation

Victoria's state government has taken a proactive stance in removing level crossings. In 2015, the Level Crossing Removal Authority was launched with the aim of removing 75 dangerous and congested level crossings across Melbourne by

2025. At the time of writing, 29 level crossings have been removed, and fifteen stations have been rebuilt.

In early 2019 work began on removing that problematic crossing in Reservoir; it has now been demolished to make way for the construction of a new above-ground rail bridge, complete with lifts and stairs for pedestrian access.

Similarly, there's been investment across the border in NSW. In the last year the Australian Rail Track Corporation delivered level crossing safety works to the value of $1.6 million across the NSW network. The focus has been on minor works such as covering road surface renewals, sighting distance improvement, renewing pedestrian level crossings, and installing CCTV monitoring at level crossings.

But is this really enough? And are politicians tapping into the public's legitimate concerns over level crossings and using them for their own gain?

A political football

While individual state governments are prioritising the removal of crossings, it's fair to say that federal government support has been lagging somewhat — until the run up to the 2019 elections.

Just weeks before the federal election, the federal treasurer Josh Frydenberg weighed in to state government affairs in what seemed to be a pretty desperate bid to save his own seat of Kooyong. Frydenberg pledged to spend $260 million on upgrading the rail system in Kooyong if he was re-elected — and he was.

Whether the Victorian government will go on to give their backing to this remains to be seen, and as I write this is still being debated. It's worth keeping in mind that even if the state government agree, Kooyong is just one area of the state of Victoria. Upgrading the rail system In Kooyong is a partial solution to what is a long-term problem for many other crossings in Victoria.

If we take a look behind us into the not-so-distant past, we see that level crossing removals have been core themes for the Victorian Labor government in the last two state elections. While the list of level crossing removals continues to be ticked off, it must be noted that it's been an expensive and painful process, causing huge disruption for commuters. Commuters are, of course, the ones who continue to weather this storm.

Fixing this broken system has to be more than a political football.

Some thoughts

I believe there are two main issues at play here: the removal or replacement of rail crossings, and the need to improve safety levels at existing crossings.

The success of issue one requires committed and strong infrastructure, and it must be backed up by investment. New rail stations need to built either above or below ground.

This needs to be paired with issue two: practical, manageable and well-thought out preventative safety measures.

The truth is, level crossings run with one simple rule: the road user has to give way to trains. That's it. Almost all the collisions that occur at rail crossings are the result of the road user failing to obey this rule. Along with this, pedestrians need to be fully aware of the dangers of crossings.

To that end, safety measures should include clear signage, loud speakers and warning lights, and a focus on pedestrian education. This needs to be addressed as soon as possible.

There's no escaping that fixing these problems nation-wide is a complex task. There are many standards that impact the safety of level crossings including the National Rail Safety Act, the State Rail Safety Act, and Workplace Standards. These differing standards then lead to different practices between the states — creating confusion.

Interestingly, there's a process that's in play at the moment to align the standards nationally, with any serious accidents at level crossings being nationally investigated.

The bottom line is that level crossing removals require planned infrastructure, *and* they require preventative safety, *and* they require pedestrian education. A coordinated effort between state and federal government is required — and it needs to go beyond an eleventh hour election pledge. Solid commitment is essential to create change and to facilitate the fixing of these broken, outdated and ultimately dangerous crossings.

Notre Dame: Some Thoughts On Her Resurrection

We're back to buildings now — albeit an extraordinary and sacred one. In April 2019, a fierce fire ravaged through The Cathedral of Notre Dame in Paris, leaving France, and the rest of the world, in shock.

The cathedral was undergoing renovation when a blaze accidentally started, devastating — but not completely destroying — the holy building. Famed for its Gothic architecture, Notre Dame is dear to France, to Catholics, and to admirers world-wide.

Its historical significance can't be underestimated: construction began almost 850 years ago, and it would be a further 200 years before it was complete. Isn't it incredible to think that the first people who started bringing this building to life wouldn't be around to see it finished?

To get a sense of the magnificence of Notre Dame, consider this: though it was built in the 12th Century, the solid timber oaks, sourced from nearby forests and used in the construction, were planted in the 7th century. It's a huge part of European, if not world-wide, history.

It's not surprising that in the aftermath of the fire, donations to restore the church flooded in from around the world — with close to a billion euros raised in a matter of weeks.

At the time of writing, work has begun on the resurrection of Our Lady of Notre Dame, with France's president, Emmanuel Macron, citing that he hopes the work will be completed in five years. Is this achievable, or overly ambitious? And if it is completed in five years, will there be a cost to its authenticity?

Let's look at this case in closer detail. We'll start by taking into account how Notre Dame was built, how the fire has affected her, and we'll look to similar buildings that have been resurrected in recent history to give us an indication of what it will take to save this sacred building.

Medieval Europe: a time of building ingenuity

As you might expect, there wasn't much variety in terms of available building materials in the 12th Century. What was available was heavy — principally stone — so designers and builders needed to find innovative ways to create these monumental structures. The only light weight available was timber, so engineering ingenuity and experimentation with structural design were essential.

We can see evidence of this ingenuity clearly in

Notre Dame, in particular with the six-part stone domes which characterise the ceiling. The pressure of the domes, along with the outward pressure on the walls, held the roof and the ceilings in place.

In order to get additional height on top of the domed stone structures, local timbers from nearby forests were used. These were large twelve by twelve inch beams, with even larger timbers running through the top of the building.

The flying buttresses that branch out from side of the Cathedral act as stone arms and they marry in with the stone vaults inside. This ensures the outward pressure from the stone vault doesn't push the walls out and buckle them; instead they're kept firmly in place.

Monumental buildings like Notre Dame are key examples of this period of innovative and interesting design. For me, they're extra awe-inspiring when we consider the time and constraints under which they were built.

Fighting the flames: what the firefighters were faced with in April 2019

It's important to acknowledge that very old buildings, and this was true of Notre Dame, don't have deliberate firestops. In other words, they're not fitted with the fireproofing elements we incorporate today into our buildings to impede the spread of fire and smoke. However, Notre Dame had an accidental fire stop — and it saved a good portion of the building. We'll get to that in a moment.

First, let's keep in mind that a fire needs three things to burn: fuel, heat, and oxygen. If one of these components is removed, the fire can be slowed down or controlled — but while ever all three are present, the fire will ravage on.

Let's look at each component in turn to get a better

sense of what the firefighters were facing and dealing with as they battled to save Notre Dame.

Fuel

Given that the fire started higher up in the building, a major source of fuel came from those old timber oaks. These were hard, if not impossible, to remove from the fire as they were prevalent throughout the ceiling and the roof of the church. It's important to note that those timbers had been drying out for over a thousand years, making them highly flammable.

In the early stages of the fire it may have been possible to cut the fuel source by cutting a trench from the gutter to the apex, and down to the other side of the gutter. If this had been done on two sides of the roof, the fire could have been contained — but the truth is the fire was too far gone for this to be an option for the firefighters.

Oxygen

Think of those high valued ceilings common in every church. They're open, airy, and oxygenated. That's fantastic for Sunday worship, giving that awe inspiring feeling when the light shines in through the stained-glass windows into the open area and light-filled space.

But in a fire situation, a high vaulted ceiling is space for an immense amount of oxygen — and that's very hard to control and shut down.

Heat

The truth is, the fire was too high up and powerful to control the heat with water. Aerial waterways or telescopic booms to shoot the water up to the roof might have been an option, but the roof was too high to be able to do that.

So what options did the firefighters have? None,

other than to go inside the building with their two and a half inch hoses, and do all they could reach the top of that fire and control it. That's a real challenge when you've got those heavy, massive lengths of timber falling down and crumbling around you. Along with that, there was the added burden of taking out the priceless artworks and saving whatever they could of the church — all the while trying, somehow, to get that fire under control.

So what saved the church from being totally destroyed? That accidental fire stop — in the shape of those six-part domes that were a feature of the experimentation of the medieval building period.

Those vaulted ceiling areas stopped the fire from spreading and helped to control it and keep the walls in place, after both the roof and the spire had burnt off.

They stopped the fire spreading into the next chamber and into the main part of the church, and they kept the walls in place with their link to the flying buttresses on the outside. And that's what saved Notre Dame.

The resurrection of Notre Dame

This will undoubtedly be a monumental project, and a hard one to tackle. While the structural elements can be replicated, there are a few questions to juggle. Essentially, it's about balancing the use of medieval style construction with modern knowledge, techniques, and technology we have available to us now. The first step is assembling the team with right know-how to do it.

Getting the right teams together and in place

A normal building project has a huge team of designers and construction experts, along with local council authorities. With Notre Dame, that team needs to include historians, authorities from the church, and specialists who have an understanding of the history of the structure.

Understandably, a lot of old buildings don't necessarily have detailed blueprints or plans to work from, so the engineers, architects, historians, and trades people will have to work out how to slowly and meticulously put everything back in place. It's also necessary to have the right people on board to document the design, and to document the actual reconstruction of such a huge endeavour.

How long will it take?

That's a big question. A project like this isn't just about the refurbishment and restoration — it's a whole conservation measure. As we've stated, Notre Dame is 850 years old, a symbol of France, a symbol of Gothic medieval architecture — and a UNESCO heritage site. In my opinion, the conservation measures alone will take about two years.

Emmanuel Macron's pledge to complete the restoration in five years is a possibility, assuming that the right teams are ready and able to get in and get the job done, but the truth is — to get it back to absolute authenticity, it's very likely it'll take a lot longer.

Other instances of church fires around the world have taken closer to 20 to 25 years to be brought back to their original state. I'll speak more about the work carried out on these buildings as we move through this chapter.

First, let's look at the kind of questions and considerations those tasked with brining Notre Dame back to life are facing.

Ensuring structural integrity and safety

After an incident such as this, top of the list of priorities is to check the structural integrity of the building. At Notre Dame the fire left the roof open and the church exposed to the elements. Though the walls are in place, they'll need to be stabilised with shoring, scaffolding and bracing.

Next, it's important to ascertain whether or not it's safe for the public to go in to the church while work is carried out on the restorations. From my experience with working on buildings that have suffered fires on a smaller scale, I'd recommend keeping the public away while restoration efforts are in progress. It's just not safe.

Furthermore, there have been initial reports of potential lead contamination and lead pollution. With approximately 3000 tons of lead in the roof and steeple, it's essential to keep people as far away from the site as possible during the early stages of renovation.

The truth is, it isn't until the teams enter a building like this and start slowly investigating that they can determine where the actual risks and dangers are.

Testing

Luckily, none of the historic stained glass in the windows of Notre Dame was damaged. When a similar gothic building, York Minster in the UK, suffered a huge fire in 1984, close to 7000 pieces of stained glass cracked — so it seems Notre Dame has been lucky to escape that same fate.

The stone, however, is going to need some serious testing. The incredible amount of heat that went through the building can't be underestimated. That heat causes a whole lot of thermal shock, and the affected areas will be then be exposed to the cold, the rain, and other elements which could lead to the stone cracking.

Core samples of the areas that have been affected by the fire should be taken and compared with core samples of the areas that have not. This will help to ascertain which parts of the church are salvageable and which aren't.

In 2016, St. Sava's Cathedral in New York City suffered a similar fire to the one at Notre Dame. In this case, the entire roof burnt down, and the inside was destroyed too. Now, only the walls remain. They're being held up by scaffolding and supports, while the church is being slowly and meticulously rebuilt.

What's salvageable?

When a huge fire ripped through The Chapel of the Holy Shroud in Turin, Italy, in 1997, it had already been closed for seven years after a large piece of marble feel from a cornice. After the fire, over 4000 pieces of original architectural elements were salvaged, but 1150 of those pieces weren't able to be used or repaired.

Incredibly, renovators sourced marble from the local quarry where the original marble was mined over 300 years before. Blueprints were re-engineered — or reverse engineered — by looking at the existing building, and the marble was slowly and meticulously put back in place. Such care was taken, even to the extent of matching the grains of the newly sourced marble with the existing marble.

The restoration of The Chapel of the Holy Shroud took over 20 years, and that wasn't as big a project as the one that the teams renovating Notre Dame are faced with. In cases like this, renovators are essentially reverse engineering the whole thing and building out of the rubble. It's an incredible feat.

At Notre Dame, similar decisions will be made around what's salvageable from the original elements, and how to remove and take care of those original elements.

From there, discussions can begin on how to rebuild areas that require rebuilding, and this is where issues and questions around authenticity will come in.

How authentic is authentic?

There will be two big questions on the table as the restoration of Notre Dame gets underway: how to source the material to rebuild the lost elements — and what techniques to use.

The choice will be between using skilled artisans and tradespeople who understand how to hand-build (York Minster is a prime example of utilising crafts people in their restoration efforts), or taking advantage of the modern technology available today.

A church in New York City, Saint John the Divine, used state-of-the-art technology to build similar structural elements to Notre Dame after suffering a fire in 2001.

The crux of it is this: the process of rebuilding by hand versus using modern technology and materials will make a massive difference in time and money.

Next, there's the question of whether modern elements should be added to the church, particularly when it comes to safeguarding and protecting it into the future.

For example, the timber from those local forests planted in the 7th Century were a significant part of the character and history of Notre Dame. Something like 13,000 trees were felled for the build, so will that be replicated on the same scale? If so, it'll be quite a challenge. And even though timber would add to the authenticity of the restoration, we can't ignore the fact that it was timber which acted as fuel for the fire.

Is it worth the risk? Or should a different type of material, such as structural steel, be used to support the roof? And what about sprinkler systems?

The fact is that a lot of those timbers were hidden above the stone vaulted ceiling, so they're not actually visible to visitors and worshippers who come into the church. Without going in and seeing it first hand myself, my hunch would be that it would be possible to hide most of those new structural elements within the stone vaulted ceiling and still keep the integrity of the church.

It's here where we loop back to the question of authenticity: there's always a call for original materials and original design in order to keep everything as close to what the building originally was. It's a matter of balance, while keeping an eye on the future as well as the past of this historic building.

What's the cost?

This will be dependent on the level of authenticity and the methods used to rebuild. Again, it comes down to absolute authenticity in the entire building — versus using a better balance of modern materials and designs to ensure the building is protected from future fires.

It's important here to be mindful that Notre Dame, and historic buildings like her, are living things. This is not the first time that Notre Dame has had retrofitting or refurbishments done. She's lived a long life to here, from surviving the French Revolution, to garnering more attention after Victor Hugo's novel in the 1840s. She oversaw the coronation of Napoleon, and she underwent those recent renovations that were in progress when this fire broke out. Now, as she's restored and brought back to life after the fire, there's an international competition inviting architects to design the spire that was lost in April 2019.

In this way, buildings are living things which change throughout time — and if Notre Dame survives another 850 years, this fire, as devastating as it may be, will become part of her story.

Three Gas Leaks, Two Very Different Outcomes, A lot of Lessons Learned

In April 2019, 500 people were safely evacuated from the Sydney Opera House after an excavator hit a gas main during construction works. Much to the credit of the construction team and the safety crew, all of the necessary safety procedures were followed — but how close was this leak to becoming a major catastrophe?

Accidentally damaging any utility, whether it's water, electricity, or gas is serious – and it's serious because essential services are interrupted, repairs are costly, and safety crews and the general public are put at risk.

Natural gas is extremely combustible. In large enough quantities it can be explosive and deadly.

Escaping gas can migrate to nearby areas and buildings — and from there it can ignite in minutes.

What causes gas leaks?

The number one cause of gas leaks is faulty, decaying, or unmaintained pipe lines. The second most common cause comes as a result of excavation incidents — and that's what happened at the Opera House.

Leaking gas will always take the path of least resistance; and that might be through a water or sewer pipe, or even through the space between a tree root and surrounding soil. In short, the gas will find any available conduit or channel to travel through.

An open excavation allows gas to escape into the outside air where it will rise and vent into the atmosphere, helping it to dissipate from the site of a leak. This makes it relatively less dangerous, and this is the case with the leak at the Opera House.

But let's take a look at some similar situations that, sadly, were far more tragic. We'll then move on to explore the lessons learnt from these incidents, and the measures put in place to protect against them in the future.

In Harlem, New York, 2014, a huge explosion from a natural gas leak killed eight people, injured at least 70 others, and displaced an estimated 100 families. The explosion was so big it levelled two five-storey buildings. In this case, officials attributed the leak to that number one cause of gas leaks: faulty and badly maintained gas pipes.

But perhaps one of the most notorious cases in recent times was the 2010 pipeline explosion in San Bruno, California, which resulted in the death of eight people and caused dozens of injuries. Officials concluded that the explosion was triggered by an electrical issue at a control centre some 60 kilometres away from the blast site.

This electrical issue caused the valves that regulate the pipeline pressure to open up, allowing more gas into the line. As the pressure increased, substandard welding in a section of the pipe ruptured and ripped open. A massive quantity of gas escaped, erupting into a huge pillar of fire. To understand the scale of the quantity of escaped gas, know that it was enough to run 12,000 homes for a year.

Lessons learnt

How can we learn from these devastating and destructive events? How can the Australian Pipe Line and Gas Association (or APGA) who are responsible for overseeing Australia's pipeline infrastructure, ensure that we're protected from risk at the hands of leaks like the one we had at the Opera House?

In San Bruno, after six years of investigations and proceedings, the company responsible for the pipeline, Pacific Gas and Electric Company (or PG&E), was convicted of six criminal charges in relation to that 2010 incident. Punishments included a three million dollar fine, a five year probation period, independent safety monitoring, and 10,000 hours of community service.

It's also essential that we look beyond punishment, and observe the measures that have been implemented not only by PG&E, but which have also been recognised and incorporated by other gas companies — all with the end goal of ensuring something like this won't happen again. These measures include restructuring the gas operations business, and hiring the best natural gas experts in the country to run the operations.

Further to this, PG&E put over 3500 of their leaders and managers, of various levels, through safety training. They also reviewed the lessons of San

Bruno with every single new employee. They conducted advanced pipeline safety testing and replaced extensive amounts of pipe; this included decommissioning more than 1000 kilometres of cast-iron pipe with stronger, more efficient and earthquake-ready pipe.

Additionally, they also installed over 200 automated and remotely controlled emergency shut-off valves. They built a new gas operations control centre to better monitor the entire system, allowing them to respond quickly and effectively to any emergencies.

Finally, PG&E upgraded all of their gas leak detection technology. It's now 1000 times more sensitive than before — meaning they can find and fix any leaks before they become a problem.

Key take-aways

These incidents and the way they were dealt with in the aftermath highlight the importance of maintaining and upgrading our pipeline infrastructure, of fixing broken or ineffective systems, and being willing to constantly test and improve our emergency response systems.

If we can proactively implement and maintain ongoing improvements to our systems we can learn from — and avoid — further tragic and fatal accidents like the ones at San Bruno 2010 and New York 2014.

In this way, we have the power to stop and control future accidents before they even happen, minimising the risk of any single incident becoming catastrophic. Let's make a pact to always be willing to learn from our mistakes.

Mascot Towers:
Cracks And Controversy

June 2019 saw the second evacuation of a Sydney residential tower in just six months. The ten-storey Mascot Towers, near Sydney's international and domestic airports, were evacuated after an engineer raised concerns over the safety of the building. Cracks were discovered in a slab transfer beam supporting a primary building corner — cracks that had suddenly increased in size, indicating there'd been some building movement in the basement area.

Unsurprisingly, this observation called for further investigation in order to determine the full risk and remedy required for this situation.

What is a slab transfer beam?

High-rise buildings and multi-storey developments, especially those with large podiums, often require additional structural stability to handle the excessive weight of the building.

In order to transfer the load and weight of a high-rise to the supporting columns, including the perimeter and corner columns going through to the foundations, a huge tabletop slab with inbuilt concrete beams is constructed. This table-top slab, known as a transfer slab or transfer beam, is made out of concrete and reinforced with steel bars and post-tensioned tendons. The complex undertaking is one of the most important tasks in the construction of a multi-storey building — and it was in the slab transfer beam where the cracks were discovered at Mascot Towers.

Acting on the engineer's advice, the Tower's building manager contacted emergency services who took the step of evacuating the building.

Meanwhile engineers worked to provide answers regarding the state of the building, and the risks involved for the residents.

How real was the risk?

In essence, the engineers were worried that the cracks could cause movement in the apartment complex, and while reports seemed to indicate that the cracks weren't massive — in fact they weren't wide enough to allow a finger to fit in — it's worth remembering the cracks were in the slab transfer beam, which, as we've covered, supports and transfers a balanced proportion of the load of the structure of the building.

Furthermore, this wasn't the first time that structural issues had been brought to the attention of the owners, residents, and managers at Mascot Towers. Several weeks prior to this incident, the owners corporation had noticed and reported on cracks in the basement. Engineers were brought in to investigate, and it was widening of these cracks which contributed to the call for the building to be evacuated. Furthermore, one resident said the problems with cracks had been going on for years, and that repairs had been scheduled for the end of 2019.

It's clear that the evacuation was a response to an ongoing and persistent cracking and structural issue in the primary support structure. With that in mind, I believe there *was* valid reason to be concerned, and given that this deterioration was rapid, propping was quickly installed as a precaution to ensure the safety of the building and its occupants.

Controversy and conflicting reports

The evacuation has, of course, left the residents of all 122 units effectively homeless after they where given just one hour to evacuate. Worse, it was late in the evening, and some residents were unaware of what was happening until they returned from work, or dinner, only to be denied access to their unit.

As is often the case with situations like this, the real risk will no doubt unfold in time, but it must be noted that in the immediate aftermath there was some conflicting information about how safe or unsafe the building was.

This stemmed from the fact that one of the residents, a man named Mr Ang, was somehow missed in the evacuation process. Waking the next morning to find himself in an empty apartment block, Mr Ang went on to question why he'd been allowed to stay in an apparently unsafe structure. He told reporters that he felt scared, confused and alone after authorities failed to check his apartment, simply leaving him to sleep as everybody else fled.

However, both the police spokesperson and NSW Fire and Rescue Superintendent Adam Dewberry stated that there was no immediate risk of the building collapsing, and that therefore Mr Ang was not in any danger. "At no time was he in danger of the building collapsing," said Dewberry.

Naturally, this conflicting information has caused frustration and left a question mark over why the building was evacuated in the first place. After all, concrete shrinks, cracks appear, and buildings move (some more than others), so it's easy to see why this frustration is there, especially for the residents. But once again, I do believe that in this case the authorities, the engineer and the building manager did the right thing by evacuating the building. Safety should always be the first priority.

Assessments are now being made by engineers and emergency management teams, including government agencies. There's still an insistence that there's no concern about any catastrophic failure or collapse — so hopefully Mascot Towers can be stabilised and the issues resolved quickly, with the residents allowed to come back to their homes as soon as possible.

What caused this problem?

There's speculation that a new building next door, which is not yet occupied, could be the culprit. During its construction several residents made complaints that Mascot Towers shook. The build was completed a month before this incident occurred.

Local state member Ron Hoenig curiously noted that Mascot Towers has been up for twelve years — now all of a sudden there are substantial cracks in the structure. He also noted that state rail engineers inspected the damage and said there's no impact at all to the Mascot Railway Station, which runs underneath the complex.

Naturally, there's a lot of speculation after an event like this, and often the finger of blame is pointed at the builder. It seems like a logical conclusion to assume something went wrong in the construction process — but it's not always the case.

High-rise towers are very complex structures, with different layers and levels of expertise involved in the whole process. It's essential that these teams and individuals work together at every stage to ensure a successful build. And, as I stated earlier in the book, issues with broken buildings are about more than just the build stage. There's that trio of areas: design, build and maintain, which we need to consider together, not in isolation.

The design process is just as complex — oftentimes even more complex — than the building process. This is when the architects and engineers create the design and decide on the structural, geotechnical and other elements that have to work together to build this structure.

Next, the builder takes what is essentially a huge

recipe book so to speak, and begins to bring it to life as per the engineers and architects instructions.

This should be a collaborative process where all parties — who are all respective experts in their field — work together by providing feedback and cross checking each others' works to ensure that they're appropriate, that they'll perform as intended, and that together they're creating a healthy building.

Once a build is complete, it needs to be maintained, just as a car requires regular servicing and due care.

If one or more of these three key elements: design, build and maintain, are lacking — the building will have issues.

Master Builders Association executive director Brian Seidler acted as a welcome voice of reason after the Mascot Towers evacuation and investigation. He noted that it's too early to tell what the cause of the problem is, because there's still a whole lot of pieces of this puzzle yet to be uncovered. We have to be mindful, before a proper call can be made, of all components — from the engineer who played a role in the design of the building, to the architect, to the builder and the developer, and finally to those who were responsible for how the building was managed and maintained.

Let's hope that whatever is occurring at Mascot Towers can be resolved quickly, with lessons learned and assurances of future safety for all concerned.

Bridge Construction:
How Can We Stop These Structures From Collapsing?

In August 2018, tragedy struck Northern Italy when a portion of the Ponte Morandi Bridge in Genoa collapsed, killing 43 people and injuring sixteen more. Rather than repair the bridge, the decision was taken to demolish it — a process that has just been completed at the time of writing — in preparation for it to be rebuilt.

The terrible tragedy of Ponte Morandi has served as a startling reminder of how essential it is that engineers, construction workers and inspectors ensure bridges are deigned, built and maintained correctly.

I'll be taking a closer look at what went wrong at Ponte Morandi soon, but first let's get a wider picture about the current state of bridges around the world.

According to the Global Infrastructure Hub, the world faces an incredible 15 trillion US dollar gap between the estimated investment and the amount needed to provide adequate infrastructure across the world by 2040.

Bridges are a fundamental part of that necessary infrastructure, and with a growing concern in recent years about the condition of bridges, it's a very pressing issue.

Beyond aesthetics

A bridge represents more than an iconic image on a city skyline. Sydney Harbour Bridge is, from a tourist's point of view, a beautiful landmark, but it's also vital to our country's economy, and essential for the transport of goods and people going to and from the economic hub of Sydney. If any bridge collapses or is damaged, the result is major chaos for the economy in the local area, and of course — potential loss of human life and severe injuries. So it's absolutely vital that bridges are designed and built with a high level of professionalism, skill and integrity.

It's also essential that the right steps are taken to protect and preserve bridges once they're in use to ensure that they fulfil their role of facilitating transport and trade — and of doing that in a way that instills confidence and a sense of safety and security in using these complex structures.

The Ponte Morandi Collapse

Designed by Riccardo Morandi, the bridge took four years to construct, opening in September 1967, and costing a staggering seven billion dollars to build. It acted as a road viaduct on the motorways along one of the major links from Italy to France.

In terms of its design, it was a cable-stayed bridge, meaning it used towers to run cables, and those towers and cables supported the deck of the bridge to hold it in position.

In the aftermath of the collapse, it transpired that the cause came down to the corrosion of these cable stays, pointing to the fact it was maintenance — or lack of — that leas this bridge to fall. When the corroded cable stays lost their ability to support the bridge, the structure began to collapse, resulting in the tragic loss of lives of those unsuspecting commuters.

The disaster caused political controversy about the poor state of infrastructure in Italy, and it also raised concerns about the condition and safety of bridges across the world.

I'd like to go back into the past a little now and into our own backyard here in Australia — where we know all too well that the issue with bridge construction is far from a new problem.

West Gate Bridge

In October 1970 we experienced one of the worst construction catastrophes Australia has ever seen when the half-built West Gate Bridge in Melbourne came crashing down.

A 100 metre span of this partially-built bridge collapsed into the Yarra River in Melbourne killing 35 construction workers, some who were working on the structure at the time it fell, and others who were taking their lunch break in the huts under the bridge.

This 2000 tonne construction plummeted into the river with an explosion of gas, dust and mangled metal. Such was the force of the collapse that buildings hundreds of metres away shook and nearby houses were spattered with mud. The impact was so loud that the sound of the collapse, the explosion, and the fire that followed it, was heard over 20 kilometres away.

Immediately after the collapse, a royal commission was set up to investigate the cause. Concluding in 1971, it cited that the bridge had fallen for two reasons: firstly the structural design, and secondly what was described as an unusual method of construction that the contractors had taken.

Construction of the bridge started again a year later, and the bridge was finally completed in 1978. This cable-stayed bridge is worth 202 million dollars and acts as a vital link between Melbourne's Central Business District and the western suburbs — and it's one of the busiest road corridors in Australia.

Galloping Gertie

Let's go even further back in time and take a look at a construction that you'd think would inspire us to do more to salvage the state of the world's bridges: possibly the biggest and most famous non-fatal engineering disaster in American history.

In Washington, 1938, construction on the Tacoma Narrows Bridge started: a suspension bridge that spanned the Tacoma Narrows strait of Puget Sound between Tacoma and the Kitsap Peninsula.

During construction, it was noted that the bridge moved vertically in windy conditions — somewhat like a galloping horse — earning it the nickname Galloping Gertie. Even when the construction of the bridge was completed in July 1940, and it was open for public use, the problem hadn't been resolved.

Measures were taken to try to stop the bridge from moving, but all proved ineffective. The bridge's main span finally gave way and completely collapsed in the face of strong winds — just five months after it was first opened in November of 1940.

The collapse of Galloping Gertie had a lasting effect on science and engineering, and it's still used now as a case study in many physics and engineering and construction books. The collapse also encouraged new research into bridge construction, research from lessons learnt in failure, and research that's influenced the designs of all long-span bridges designed and built after Galloping Gertie.

Let's widen our lens now and explore what actually causes a bridge to collapse.

Five main reasons that bridges collapse

1. Environment and climate

Climate variations can have a huge impact on the materials used in bridge construction. When a bridge is being designed, it's essential that the specific conditions of the climate are taken into account. Further to that, once that bridge is up we also need skilled and qualified inspectors to identify signs of degradation caused by the climate, and to identify areas which need to be fixed, maintained or remedied. That way, measures to replace cracking and corroding can be taken care of, and risks and weakness in the structure can be identified.

2. Stress and fatigue

Bridges are subject to wear and tear, not just from the climate, but from general use. The constant pressure of the sheer number of vehicles that pass over a bridge, in particular heavy trucks and transport vehicles, has to be taken into account. This stress and fatigue from vehicles is common on

suspension and cable-stayed bridges, so it's vital
that inspectors regularly check for signs that a
bridge is suffering from fatigue.

3. Inadequate funding

It goes without saying that in order to inspect and
maintain bridges, we need adequate funding to do
the job. We need a budget in place that allows us to
find the real issues, report them clearly and put the
teams together to do the works to maintain the
bridges, including enough money in the pot to
complete bridge upgrades over time. Sometimes
authorities don't have access to the required
resources, but the simple fact is a lot of time and
effort from skilled engineers is required to ensure
the safety and the upgrading of an ageing bridge —
and that requires money.

4. Design defects

Frustrating as it is, some bridges were destined to

collapse due to issues and shortfalls in design. If a design hasn't fully considered environmental conditions, or if there's a structural flaw, that design was doomed to failure from the moment it was put down on a blueprint.

5. Poor maintenance

Poor maintenance is a difficult problem to diagnose following a bridge collapse. We know that many, many bridge collapses could have been prevented with more stringent inspections and well-planned and thought out maintenance routines. Even when collapses happen for other reasons — those collapses are simply exacerbated by poor maintenance.

Looking to the future

What can we do to manage the trio of design, construction and maintenance in our infrastructure to prevent more of our bridges collapsing?

Let's look to America, a country leading the way with innovative infrastructure developments, particularly in areas that are at high risk of earthquakes, such as San Francisco.

The San Francisco-Oakland Bridge, better known as the Bay Bridge, is a self-anchored suspension bridge that stretches 13.5 kilometres to unite San Francisco and Oakland.

In 1989 the bridge was damaged by a severe earthquake, a tremor so strong that the whole 220 tonne section of the bridge's east span collapsed. The scale of the damage was so bad that officials decided to replace the entire span. Designers and engineers set themselves an ambitious goal: to build a new bridge that would be quake-proof.

After almost a decade of work, and over six billion dollars, the bridge was reopened in 2013, but it wasn't just repaired and rebuilt — it was also constructed with special components that allowed it to withstand the next earthquake.

According to the California Department of Transportation, engineers used "rock motions" which calculate the maximum seismic forces the bridge would experience. This, combined with huge leaps in technological advancements in recent years, could be the essential ingredients to preventing bridges from collapsing.

What other methods do we have at our disposal?

Advanced monitoring systems can be used to detect the state of a bridge on an ongoing basis, with fibre optic sensors to examine the changes in fibre properties when a structure comes under strain. The system sends light signals through optical fibres to look into the health of a bridge. The sensors are embedded right inside the bridge or attached to the bridge.

We can also use small electronic and mechanical systems, or micro systems, that collect the measurements of structures, along with GPS, to measure bridge movements by tracking the location of strategically placed GPS transmitters.

Finally, non-contact measurement techniques can also be used to capture the structural changes of a bridge. Cameras can be installed to capture images of a bridge, and those images can be analysed using image processing techniques.

But monitoring the health of a bridge isn't just about collecting measurements. The biggest challenge is to make sense of the data and then use that expert knowledge to provide reliable reports on bridge health that we can act on.

It's a dynamic process, a process that requires expertise to use the knowledge we have to improve the safety of bridges. In essence, regular inspections, an innovative mindset, the willingness to embrace new technology and continuous monitoring all work together to minimise the possibility of catastrophic accidents — and to keep the economy, and traffic — flowing safely.

The Combustible Cladding Crisis

It's not an understatement to say that combustible cladding has become a major cause for concern within the Australian construction industry. Thousands of buildings across the country continue to be identified as having high-risk and potentially flammable cladding on their exteriors, and the government is yet to devise a conclusive national solution to what is a truly disastrous situation.

The true horrors of combustible cladding were brought to life in Australia when the Lacrosse Tower fire broke out in Melbourne in 2014. It took just eleven minutes for the fire to travel up thirteen floors and reach the roof of the tower block. Thankfully, no lives were lost.

Three years later, in 2017, the world watched in horror as the 24-storey Grenfell Tower in London became engulfed in deadly flames. There's no doubt the harrowing images of the raging fire that killed 72 people will be forever etched in our minds. But it was the Neo200 apartment fire in Spencer Street, Melbourne, in February this year, that proved a stark reminder that not enough is being done to ensure the safety of our buildings — and those who reside within them.

State governments across New South Wales, Queensland and Victoria have been forced to take action. We'll explore those measures in a moment, and we'll also ask — are they enough? And what are the consequences of the cladding crisis — for the industry, and for owners and residents?

A closer look at cladding

Cladding itself is the process of overlaying the exterior of a building with panels that improve insulation, provide some resistance to weather, and improve the building's appearance.

Not all cladding is highly flammable. Cladding is only considered combustible when the material it's made of, or the process used to design it, has a high risk of igniting. In other words, when the cladding will catch fire easily, leading to the fire spreading very, very quickly.

Because cladding runs up the exterior of the building in a vertical layout, it only takes something like a discarded cigarette on a balcony to start a fire that will rapidly take off and spread to the floors above. This was the cause of the Neo200 tower fire in February 2019. Terrifyingly, the fire spread from the 22nd to the 27th floor in a matter of minutes.

Negligence or misunderstanding?

Interestingly, building managers at the Neo200 claimed that the complex was deemed fully compliant with cladding standards when it was inspected in 2017.

Even more startlingly, a recent audit by the Victorian Building Authority (VBA) found that over 1400 buildings across the state contained high-risk combustible cladding, putting the spotlight on failings at the design, approval, and construction levels of the build.

The VBA's Chief Executive stated that this clearly highlighted "a misunderstanding" of the requirements of the national construction code. As a result, stakeholders and owners have called for better education surrounding the code requirements and a restructuring of the code itself.

From my point of view, it's essential that the codes are developed so that there's no room for misinterpretation or lack of understanding: the safety of our society depends on this.

Small steps: what are the state governments doing?

Since the most recent spate of fires, most state governments have tightened their regulations around cladding.

In New South Wales, it's now a legal requirement that the owners of mixed-use or residential buildings higher than two storeys and with exteriors that include combustible cladding, register the building with the New South Wales Government. This includes cladding constructed of metal composite panels that contain aluminium, zinc, and copper in the outer layers, as well as the inner core materials such as polythylene — which is very flammable. It also includes insulated cladding systems that are comprised of polystyrene and polyurethane, amongst others.

Further south in Victoria, the government has also issued a ban on the use of aluminium composite panels with polyethylene and expanded polystyrene cores. Tragically, cladding panels with a polyethylene core were the ones used in a refurbishment of London's Grenfell Tower, the year before the fire broke out.

In the case of Grenfell, the manufactures of the panels had actually advised customers not to use polyethylene-cored tiles on high-rise towers. Despite that advice, panels with a polyethylene core were used to refurbish the building in 2016.

How did that happen? Well, at the time building regulations in the UK didn't include an explicit ban on polyethylene core panels. In the UK many safety rules are implemented in principle rather than being mandatory, and therefore there's a reliance that companies will act with safety in mind rather than having to follow enforced regulations.

Back in Australia, New South Wales, Queensland and Victoria now require property owners to remove dangerous cladding at their own cost.

Considering the increasingly higher density living that we've been growing into, strata owners in thousands of buildings across Australia have been affected by this. Unsuspecting owners across the country have been shocked to receive letters from the state government stating that the building that they own or live in is covered in high-risk combustible cladding — and that it has to be removed at once. If the cladding isn't removed, owners are handed a fine nearing $400,000.

Who's responsible? And who's footing the bill?

As state governments continue to grapple with how best to resolve the cladding crisis, the issue of who's liable and who will have to pay to rectify the high-risk cladding is still unclear.

What is clear is that insurance companies have introduced exemptions to policies, which allow them to omit cladding from agreements. The last remaining insurer to cover cladding, Landmark Underwriting, will no longer provide cladding cover as of July 2019.

Furthermore, insurance companies have started rejecting professional indemnity insurances for building surveyors — and those surveyors are now faced with the prospect of losing their livelihood. This drastic move creates a snowball effect: businesses could be forced to shut down operations, creating costly project delays as surveyors attempt to find a solution to a seemingly impossible situation.

In essence, no registration for surveyors means no construction approvals, effectively sending the construction industry into lockdown until the matter is resolved — or possibly the government steps in.

Just imagine the number of projects affected, the impact on investors, stakeholders, and of the jobs of thousands of people. If no one steps in to fill the void in the insurance market we could see the construction industry grind to a halt as a result.

The backlash of the insurance issue has proved particularly serious in Victoria, the state with the largest known number of privately-owned buildings riddled with inflammable cladding. All registered Victorian Building Authority surveyors are required to obtain indemnity insurance in order to practice, but with the insurance now almost impossible to obtain, those surveyors could be forced out of a job.

Premier of Victoria, Daniel Andrews, has addressed the growing issue and said while the government categorically will not allow "anybody to be uninsured", he insisted there were "some steps" the state could take. Mr Andrews also told ABC that taxpayers would potentially have to pay out of their own pockets to aid the housing crisis.

"There will have to be taxpayers' money, there will

have to be government allocations," Mr Andrews told the news program. "There can potentially be some money, some, recovered from those who have done this, have basically committed these errors and have used this dodgy product."

The Victorian state budget issued earlier this year (2019) designated $160 million to remove cladding from government buildings, and in June it named Mr Andrew Cialini as Victoria's new State Building Surveyor. He'll commence duties in July 2019, with the goal of ensuring buildings are "consistently well-built, safe and fit for purpose," the Victoria Building Authority said.

This doesn't change the fact that the removal of cladding remains expensive and a national funding scheme has not yet been put in place. Naturally, some owners are calling for the Australian government to step up and foot the bill — after all the Victorian Government makes over ten billion dollars in revenue from stamp duty and land tax in one financial year — and now many of those same taxpayers are left stranded in high-risk homes that they're unable to sell or even get insurance on while this monumental problem is investigated.

If we look to the UK, we see that following the Grenfell fire, then Prime Minister Theresa May announced £200 million in funding assistance to remove and replace combustible cladding. There have been calls for our government to do the same — construction lawyer Bronwyn Weir is one such voice. So far, however, no funding has been announced, leaving home owners and investors at a massive loss.

The cost of the removal and replacement of the cladding in most of these affected buildings could go into the millions. All of the owners in one building would now face a substantial special levy if their insurance or the state government won't cover the bill – which in many cases, it won't.

It's an unfair situation where the safety of people and property is the core issue, but the owners are the ones being hounded by regulatory authorities and left in an impossible situation — unsupported, vulnerable and somehow responsible for something that isn't their fault.

What's the solution?

Victoria seems to be leading the country in handling this tenacious issue. The state government announced the Cladding Rectification Agreement scheme last year, which offers building owners low-interest loans for cladding removal.

However, not one loan has yet been granted to an owner impacted by combustible cladding in Victoria, CBD news reported last month. Why? Well, one flaw in the conception of this scheme is the fact that it's voluntary for local councils to participate — so if the council doesn't get on board, those owners who require it can't access the funds.

Some owners are understandably going down the track of taking legal action against construction companies. The problem is the abundance of "Phoenix Companies" — companies which are created for the purpose of one particular construction project, and then dissolve after the job is done. Thankfully, the government are passing new laws targeting "Phoenix companies", but it doesn't help those already affected — who are left with defunct warranties and no one to sue.

And, as we've covered — property owners with external combustible cladding have no choice but to declare the non-compliant material. This leaves owners in truly impossible situations with their properties uninsurable until the faulty cladding is replaced.

The other issue is the sheer scale of this problem. It's unprecedented in the construction industry. High-risk combustible cladding has been identified on thousands of buildings across Australia, and mandatory removal is expensive. As we've covered, there's no national funding assistance scheme to help owners and builders through the process, the very owners that should be assisted and protected in this a scenario are being forced into financial hardship.

Preventative measures

As mentioned, tighter regulations and a ban on flammable materials have been put in place, along with the requirement to register affected buildings in NSW (those buildings are also assigned a fire danger rating), and laws have been put in place to give powers to authorities in pursuing "Phoenix Companies".

We've also seen some builders leading by example, stepping up and committing to replacing combustible cladding at no cost to owners. This was the case at the Trilogi apartments, the Exo apartments in the Docklands, and Harvest apartments in Southbank Melbourne.

What else can be done?

A number of high-rise properties have built staircases on the outside of the property as a way to stop residents from becoming stuck inside should a fire arise. Another feature, which has been used in the Burj Khalifa — the tallest building in the world in Dubai — is the installation of high-power fans. The fans are designed to rid the evacuation pathway of smoke if a fire did occur.

I also believe it's imperative to assess other fire safety measures in all affected buildings — especially given the devastating impact fire can have in buildings with high risk cladding systems. As you might expect, a number of older buildings don't meet current fire safety standards, and so it's absolutely vital that buildings are updated in line with recommendations in annual fire safety inspections.

In addition to this, strata committees in affected buildings should consider policies that prevent risk, such as smoking and lighting barbecues on balconies. Committees are representing their owners' corporation, and so any reasonable preventative measure that's specific to that building should be considered — especially while combustible cladding is on the façade, for the safety of all the owners and residents.

In the long term there must be a thorough review of the national building code, and recommendations made for demystifying any commonly misunderstood or misinterpreted requirements.

The government should also instate a nation-wide program that educates builders, surveyors, fire safety inspectors and all those involved on the updated code requirements — a move that would benefit everyone.

Finally, the owners and residents stuck in this situation need some realistic and adequate funding schemes from the government, and such schemes should be mandatory for all local councils, backed by the state — and possibly also supported by the federal government as well.

As the cladding crisis escalates, many businesses and buildings face an uncertain future. It's not an exaggeration to say that the cladding crisis could plunge the development of the industry into chaos. Only time will tell what's ahead for the construction industry in Australia.

The Millennium Tower, San Fransisco

In 2017, the thirteen storey Azarita apartment tower in Egypt, dubbed "The Leaning Tower of Alexandria", toppled over and crashed into a neighbouring residential building. Miraculously, no one was hurt.

It took 21 days for the tower to be demolished, and when questions were asked about how and why this happened, it came to light that the Azarita Tower only had planning approval to be four stories high. Along with this, the support piles beneath it were woefully inadequate. The Azarita Tower actually started to lean after a neighbouring building collapsed — yes, another one! Quite clearly this scenario points to a big problem with Egypt's construction industry — especially when Alexandria alone is estimated to currently house over 14,500 unsafe buildings.

Thankfully, extreme circumstances such as these are rare. But what about when a tower is found to be leaning in a city where there's a high level of scrutiny of the construction industry? And what if that building has actually won several awards for its design and build?

I'd like to examine the case of San Francisco's infamous Millennium Tower, and how it's earned a similar nickname to its Egyptian counterpart, becoming "The Leaning Tower of San Francisco".

The Millennium Tower forms the majority of a mixed-use development at 301 Mission Street in San Francisco. It's the tallest building in the city, and at the time of its construction it was the first high-rise built in Downtown San Francisco in 20 years. To get an idea of its size and scale, bear in mind that this 58-storey tower is connected by a glass atrium to another twelve storey building, and underneath this is a five level carpark.

The building's concrete slab sits on friction piles that extend 30 metres into the earth below. The foundations of many of the nearby buildings are similar in design, with a key difference: some of their friction piles go down a lot further than the Millennium Tower's — some as far as 80 metres. This means they engage directly with the bedrock to give them additional support. Why the disparity between the depth of the friction piles? It's simply down to the variety of conditions in the earth below Mission Street and the surrounding areas.

The Millennium Tower complex was completed in 2009 and opened to residents that same year. It cost $350million to build and, as I mentioned, it's won several awards — including accolades for outstanding engineering and project management.

And yet… the Millennium Tower is both sinking and tilting.

Warning signs?

It has transpired that during the planning phase, the developers of the tower didn't submit to a peer review. As a result, the Millennium Tower wasn't put under the same scrutiny as a similar nearby building proposed by the developer Jack Myers — a proposal that was rejected by the Department of Building Inspections. Interestingly, the rejected building had the same geotechnical engineer as the Millennium Tower.

It's been alleged that the developers let some owners know the building was sinking and tilting in 2015, but it was 2016 when the public was officially notified of the problem. By then the building had already sunk almost half a metre and tilted five centimetres at the base and up to fifteen centimetres at the top of the tower.

In 2017 the building was still considered safe to occupy — despite the sinking and the tilting, and despite the subsequent damage to the foundation and the electrical systems. Then, in 2018, the tower sunk another five centimetres and the tilt at the top of the tower became even worse at 35 centimetres. Massive cracks could be seen all over the pavement surrounding the tower at ground level, as well as in the building's basement.

The problem escalated in September of that same year when residents reported hearing loud "creaking and popping" sounds. Soon after, the windows that were designed to withstand hurricane-grade winds started cracking on the 36th floor. Understandably, a lot of people are concerned about the building's "inhabitable" status and whether it's really is safe for people to stay in their apartments.

What's the cause?

As noted, the piles under the building only go 30 metres into the soil and fill below it — a huge contrast to those nearby buildings with piles driven 80 metres right down into bedrock. Over time, the soil beneath the Millennium Tower has most likely compressed and allowed the tower to settle, and that settlement causes sinking and tilting.

There's an interesting comparison to made here. The world's original and most famous leaning tower at Pisa was built on a foundation of unstable subsurface soil, causing it to begin leaning to the south when construction started on its second storey… not that the builders let that stop them from finishing the job!

They did try to compensate and counter the lean by adjusting the design northward, though they didn't have the diagnostic and building technology of today, and evidently — it wasn't enough. Without realising it, neighbouring construction projects also worked against the best efforts of those engineers working on the tower in Pisa, by further contributing to the instability of the soil foundation.

Restoration work undertaken on the tower in the late 1990's involved placing weights on the north side, while also excavating soil from below in an effort to allow the tower to somewhat level itself out and to reduce the degree of titling.

Back to San Fransisco

In recent years, there'd been some concern that the cause of the sinking and tilting tower is related to the excavation for the construction of the neighbouring Transbay Transit Centre (TTC) — though that's unlikely to be the sole cause because the problems with the Millennium Tower were allegedly reported before the construction on the TTC had even begun — problems that included the Millennium Tower already sinking 25 centimetres.

So who is to blame? Residents and owners are divided on whether or not it's the developer, the City, or the TTC. As a result, separate groups of owners are suing at least one of these parties; some are actually suing a combination of two or three of them.

The water gets muddier and the situation gets even more complicated because the City joined the fight for liability when they filed a lawsuit against the developers in 2016, claiming that they'd withheld information about the sinking problem from potential buyers. The developer denied these claims.

Finally, in March of 2017, the owner's corporation filed a lawsuit against not only the developers, but also the engineers, builders, other contractors *and* the TTC — and they're suing for 200 million dollars to cover the remediation works and the damages.

How can the Millennium Tower be saved?

A whole host of proposed plans to fix the Tower have been floated to the owners. One suggestion involved drilling up to 300 micro-piles all the way down to the bedrock starting through the building's concrete foundation. This would be accomplished by suspending one side of the building while simultaneously allowing the other side to keep sinking until it levelled itself out.

However, too many people thought this would be too intrusive and too expensive — and by expensive I mean at an estimated cost of 350 million dollars: about the same amount it cost to build the tower in the first place.

Late last year, The Millennium Tower Association submitted an application to the City's Departments of Building Inspections proposing to have 52 new piles drilled down into the bedrock, but these 52 piles would be drilled from the sidewalk on the Tower's southwest corner. This remediation plan will cost much less at 100 million dollars — but at the time of writing the application still has to pass many stages of red tape in order to be approved, so the outcome is still months away.

Why this is a particularly challenging case

The truth us, there are so many challenges in this case, least of all liability insurance. It's similar to some of the scenarios we've seen here in Australia, where the cost to fix such monumental problems can just simply blow out the developer's liability insurance as well as the insurances of the contractors involved in the project. If the TTC is found liable, then taxpayers could end up footing the bill.

Another issue is access to the currently occupied 58-storey tower. Obviously being able to get into and out of the building safely during works is a major concern to everyone involved. This also a major reason why (apart from cost) those involved would prefer the perimeter pile upgrade and not the micro pile remedy.

Assuming the proposed plan is approved, it would be preferable that the piles are drilled down through the footpaths on just one corner of the building. This would entail less impact on the public, and on the residents in general.

A potential complication with all major remediation works at this scale is the impact on the building's surrounding streets. Traffic has to be considered, and the impact on businesses and the other residents in the nearby buildings.

In essence this is a complex undertaking in more ways than one, but one big positive that comes out of scenarios like this is the insight that we gain into how we can do better in the future. With more and more of Earth's inhabitable surface becoming overcrowded and overpopulated, buildings are extending upwards now more than ever.

With that in mind, the unfortunate but interesting phenomenon of not only sinking buildings but every type of inadequate infrastructure we've covered can be of service to us, by shedding light on how we can build better, and how we can create healthier buildings in the future.

PART THREE

Is Your Building Broken? Signs That Attention Is Required

This is something of a trouble-shooting chapter where I'll introduce you to some of the most common problems that present themselves in broken buildings, and let you in on the signs that a building requires professional attention.

The three issues we'll explore are concrete defects, issues with water and leaks, and the signs of structural damage.

Concrete defects

If you notice cracks in your concrete, crumbling surfaces or blistering paint, it's very likely the concrete has spalled — and spalling concrete requires professional attention.

What is concrete spalling, and what causes it?

Spalled concrete can be serious in extreme cases, which is why it's also known as concrete cancer. It's caused when water or moisture gets into the concrete causing the reinforcing steel within it to rust. As the steel rusts it expands, displacing the concrete around it, causing it to become brittle and crack.

You know you have spalled concrete if you notice cracks in the concrete or a crumbly texture, and often orange rust is visible on the outside of the slab. If the steel reinforcement bar is exposed to the air, the deterioration will be rapid.

Is spalling dangerous?

In a nutshell, yes. Over time, and with increased exposure to the elements, untreated pieces of concrete may fall from your structure — and you don't need me to tell you the risks involved with that.

Please note: *spalling around supporting posts of balustrades or balcony railings requires urgent attention — there's not only a risk of collapse but also a good chance that moisture will enter and weaken the support's structural integrity.*

What's required to treat concrete defects?

A thorough investigation is necessary to find the cause of the damage and detail the necessary procedures for rejuvenation. Spalling must be removed and any exposed steel treated.

Once the steel has been treated (or removed and replaced) the concrete slab needs to be protected to prevent the issue occurring again. In other words, it requires effective waterproofing.

Water: Leaks and waterproofing

In general, **waterproofing defects** can be complex and hard to pin down, in both old buildings and new. Seeing water droplets in one spot doesn't mean the water is coming from straight above; often water has tracked along a beam before falling and alerting you to the fact there's a leak of some kind. This means other areas on the water's route (which you can't always see without investigating) could also be damaged. Paintwork, electrics and carpets pretty much always suffer when water gets into a building.

Recognising the problems

If you notice a water leak, it can be tempting to dismiss it or intend to deal with it later — especially if it isn't causing any damage that you can see right now. The reality, however, is that the water may be leaking into a cavity and causing mould, or contributing to concrete cancer — which in turn leads to structural damage.

Potential causes of water leaks

Because water can track down from almost anywhere, it can be hard to identify the source.

Still, there are a handful of common causes that we see on a regular basis.

Here they are:

- If your building has a flat roof, the membrane designed to act as a waterproof barrier may have been damaged or it could be ageing.

- Inadequate flashing: flashing is the material used to cover joints, valleys and edges — basically any gap where water could get through — on roofs and around windows and doors. Sometimes flashing isn't high enough and when it rains, the wind pushes water up — going against our usual instincts about the behaviour of water — and becoming the source of the leak. In other words, water might be entering the building from below where you're actually seeing it.

- Garden beds: the soil in garden beds contains salts, fertilisers and other chemicals that can be extremely corrosive, causing leaks to occur when you might not expect them. These substances can have a very serious effect on the structural integrity of the reinforcing steel in the concrete slabs of your building. As always, prevention is better than the cure — always get effective waterproofing on garden beds.

- Issues with plumbing is another major cause of leaks.

- Concrete cancer on a flat surface, such as a balcony, is another way that water gets in.

Leaking balconies are a common but serious issue. Water penetrates into the surrounding external walls and affects the units below or adjacent to the balcony. Furthermore, there's a risk of damage to electrical systems which can cause power outages and dangerous charges. And though it's rare, because the structural integrity of the balcony is being compromised, it's impossible to discount the possibility of balcony collapse.

Structural issues: The warning signs

- Cracks in the walls, internal or external, often in a step-like manner
- Walls which are sagging
- Brickwork or render that's bulging
- Rust stains on the side of the building that originate at random
- Water leaks that are hard to track (i.e. they're not coming from directly above where you're seeing water)
- Windows or doors not fitting as soundly as before
- Lintels and arch bars (above doors and windows) showing signs of rust and cracking of brickwork
- Balconies which are leaking and cracking

- Obvious one, but… large pieces of concrete are falling from the structure

What causes structural issues?

In essence: age, exposure to the elements, and sometimes poor workmanship and materials used during construction.

If you have any doubts or concerns about the health of your building, always seek the advice of an experienced remediation company.

But how do you know what to look out for when you're choosing a team to work with? Let's look at that next.

How To Choose A Remediation Company

I recommend that you look for:

- A team that has the skill and expertise to take the three-pronged approach by looking at design, build and maintenance issues in your building
- A team that will document and report clearly on the extent of any problems they find AND offer viable solutions that address those issues
- A team that always communicates clearly, and are willing to communicate with the executive committee and insurance companies so they can act on the findings
- A team that allow you the freedom to funnel your resources — including your time and energy — into what you do best — whether that's as a strata manager or something else

Bonus item: If you're a strata manager, look for a team that can also focus on viable asset management, so that, if you wish, you can differentiate your company to one that provides both strata services and real asset management — helping your company to increase their revenues, reduce their costs and grow their market share.

Dear Strata Managers: An Open Letter

I know how busy you are, how your resources are stretched. It's likely that you're responsible for 1000, maybe 1500 units, and those units are placed across dozens of buildings around town.

While you like your job and you don't shy away from the challenges of it, you recognise you have a lot to juggle: hundreds of emails a week, the daily "urgent" phone calls requesting your immediate attention, and any time the skies open and it rains you have that niggling worry that the water will get in somewhere, somehow. And too often you're right — Mrs Jones' lounge room *has* flooded. And wasn't that leak fixed last week? For the third time… this month?

Then you've got all the new legislation to keep up with, and work health and safety requirements to cover.

While a typical working day for everyone else finishes around 5pm, that's pretty much the time you've finished putting out fires for the day. That's the time when you've finally got some peace and quiet to do the other half of your job: taking care of insurance, financial management, accounts, balancing the books, and preparing reports. And then there might be an executive committee meeting to run, and you know how often those things drag out late into the night — so often ending with indecision and ambiguity.

Does that sound familiar? I feel exhausted just writing all of that on paper, and there you are — taking care of that and more on a daily basis.

As a strata manager you have a lot of hats to wear: manager, psychologist, problem solver, diplomat, peace maker, and while you've got to love people to do your job, you also have to have a thick skin to be willing to help and at the same time roll with the abuse that's often dished out.

You're on the frontline, and you're also the brains behind many decisions — as well as the trusted advisor to the executive committees.

In reality, being a strata manager is a stress few people can handle. But it can also be really rewarding, and there's a sense of pride in being someone who can pull the strings and make order out of chaos.

What if working with the right remediation company was a way to elevate a lot of stress?

How We Do It At Savil

At Savil, our speciality is strata buildings: they're complex, they have a lot of needs and requirements, and they require a team of people on board with the expertise and experience to not only maintain them, but to identify problems, and to understand the bigger picture.

We've helped over 30 strata building committees in our time, and we've also helped countless strata managers and insurance companies.

Let's take a closer look with a case study.

Imagine a mixed-use building made up of 200 residential units and some retail space. This building has the full trio of faults:

- Design issues
- Build quality issues
- Maintenance issues

Add to that a dash of bad timing with a drought ten years ago — and all the issues such a devastating weather event brings with it.

This particular build has a host of problems: leaking balconies with a design that has water running back towards the units; foundations with so much movement that cracks have become major features throughout the building; and cracks in the slabs so that when it rains, the water tracks along the cracks and leaks into the units below.

The issues are all over the place: different buildings, different ages, different committees, different designs — all with unique problems.

Imagine you're the manager of that strata building. You don't even know if you're aware of all the issues the building has, and how risky they actually are. Even if you do know the issues and the causes, you still have to find a bunch of people who can formulate the solutions correctly and know how to fix them, because the truth is — most people get it wrong.

Finally, let's say you get past all of that and you've got all the information you need. How do you then put together a team that can coordinate with each other, work on a live site in direct interaction with the public, and provide all the reporting, customer support, skill and expertise to execute the game plan?

That's what we do.

We take care of the entire project, investigating the issues, documenting and reporting on the extent of the problems, and offering viable solutions that address the issues.

We then formulate a plan with clear communication, a plan with the knowledge that will help the executive committee to act with real confidence and clarity.

In this particular case study, we installed scaffold onto the building facades. We mechanically and safely removed drummy and cracked render. We stitched walls with chemical anchors. We applied new render and paint and removed balcony tiles and repaired waterproofing. We installed new systems including paving on stands, which allows ease of access for future maintenance.

And we did it all in a live environment with hundreds of residents, with retail units and shops, with shoppers, families and medical centres.

We even supplied people in public relations roles, helpfully reducing the burden on the strata managers.

Although our business is complicated our approach is very simple.

We can give you a team that:

1. Finds the real problem

2. Reports it clearly

3. Does the work right!

And we have a key ingredient that a lot of other companies may not prioritise — more on that in the next chapter.

Customer Service: The Neglected Element of Successful Remediation Work

The construction industry isn't always regarded as a customer service industry. You might be able to get a good product, but it rarely comes with a great experience.

At Savil we just don't accept this. For us, construction *is* a service industry. Not only does the final product matter, but so does the experience for the client, our staff and everyone else we interact with.

When you go to a restaurant, it's not just to get a good meal — you want the place to be clean, you'd like the staff to be pleasant and polite and happy, you'd like to get your meal on time, and you'd like the whole dining experience to be a great one.

Construction should be no different. It's a service industry, like any other industry, and a remediation team should have the common goal to make their client's job and life easier, and to deliver a service that will help them grow.

At Savil we produce photographic and written reports that create a clear visual story for everyone affected by our works. Often, we're invading peoples' private space, and we're in close contact with the public on a daily basis. As part of our service we communicate regularly with residents via email, leaflet drops, and face-to-face contact. We inform everyone of health and safety measures, and we always have the upmost respect for property and belongings. We keep the executive committee in the loop and of course we're always on hand for the strata manager.

If the strata manager is informed and assured about what's happening, he or she is armed with all the tools they need to show their committee what's happening easily and confidently.

We maintain the role of trusted advisor. We also offer to attend any executive committee meetings, where we can run presentations to assist with educating and informing those committees on the work that's required.

If you have any questions or would like to know more about us, find us here:

Website: www.savilgroup.com.au
Email: info@savilgroup.com.au
Phone: 0400 567 989

All that remains to say is thank you for being here, and for joining me on this foray into the world of broken buildings. It's my hope that in highlighting the times we get things wrong we can increase our chances of getting it right. We have the capacity to learn and grow, and to create a safer, more sustainable future, where our buildings are designed innovatively, built flawlessly, and maintained thoroughly.

Thank you,
Dimitri Livas

Dimitri Livas is available as an Expert Speaker and Media Expert in Construction:

Topics of Discussion include:
Fixing Broken Buildings,
Creating Healthy Buildings,
Building Remedy and Repair,
Building Defects,
Construction Issues,
Construction Business,
Construction Failures,
Building Fires and Restoration,
Historical Building Conservation and Restoration,
Construction Cost Blowouts

www.dimitrilivas.com

* 9 7 8 0 9 8 7 6 3 3 8 9 7 *